CLIFFHANGERS 4

Sue Palmer
Alison Kilpatrick
Patricia McCall

Oliver & Boyd

Acknowledgments
The authors and publishers are grateful to the following for
permission to reproduce extracts from copyright works:

Angus & Robertson (UK) Ltd, from *Ash Road* by Ivan Southall
(© Ivan Southall, 1965); The Bodley Head, from *The Cartoonist* by
Betsy Byars; Clarke Irwin & Co Ltd, from *Underground to Canada* by
Barbara Smucker (© 1977); Faber & Faber Ltd, from *The Turbulent
Term of Tyke Tiler* by Gene Kemp; Hamish Hamilton Ltd, from *Freaky
Friday* by Mary Rodgers; William Heinemann Ltd, from *Grinny* by
Nicholas Fisk and *The Ghost of Thomas Kempe* by Penelope Lively;
Macmillan, London and Basingstoke, from *Cue for Treason* by Geoffrey
Trease; Oxford University Press, from *Terry on the Fence* by Bernard
Ashley (1975); and Penguin Books Ltd, from *Nothing To Be Afraid Of*
(Kestrel Books 1980, pp. 13–16, copyright © 1977, 1980) by Jan Mark.

The authors would also like to thank the children and staff of Comiston
Primary School, Edinburgh; Caddonfoot Primary School, Galashiels and
Stenwood Elementary School, Virginia, USA, for all their help; and
Jeannette Perry, Ishbel Fraser and Graham Harding, without whom
Cliffhangers could not have been written.

*Illustrated by Nancy Bryce, Peter Chapel, Donald Harley, John Harrold
and Maggie Ling*

Oliver & Boyd
Longman House
Burnt Mill
Harlow
Essex CM20 2JE

An Imprint of Longman Group UK Ltd

First published 1983
Seventh impression 1991

ISBN 0 05 003634 3

Produced by Longman Group (FE) Ltd
Printed in Hong Kong

Contents

Introduction

In *Cliffhangers* you will find extracts from ten exciting fiction books written for people of your age. There are many sorts of fiction – adventure stories, fantasy, stories set in the past or in other parts of the world, school stories, science fiction – something for everybody to enjoy. We hope that in the *Cliffhanger* extracts, and the sections called "Other Good Reads", you will find many books that you'd like to read for yourself. The "Other Good Reads" are coded with stars – one star means that it is quite an easy read, two means that it is of medium difficulty, and three stars means that it's better left to good readers. Choose books that you know you'll be able to read quite easily – then you can relax and enjoy the story. If you like a book, then it's a good idea to look for other books by the same author.

Sometimes you may be able to find the books you want in your class or school library. If not, the local lending library might have them. You can join the library by going along with an adult and asking for a membership application form. It won't cost you anything! Fiction books are arranged on library shelves alphabetically by authors' surnames. If you can't find the book, then usually it is possible to reserve it and collect it as soon as it is returned, or else the librarian can borrow it from another library. However, since all the *Cliffhanger* extracts come from paperbacks, you may want to buy them – they are fairly cheap.

Most big bookshops have children's sections where you can buy Puffins and other paperbacks. There is even a Puffin Club you can join which sends you details of the books published in Puffin and a magazine about books. Ask at your bookshop for details of this club.

Often you get more enjoyment from a book if you think about it and talk about it. You may even gain a better understanding of your own thoughts, feelings and experiences when you come across something similar in books. The discussions you are asked to take part in after each extract should help you to understand both the events and the reasons why the characters behave as they do. You will also have the chance to talk about your own experiences and your own thoughts on various subjects connected with the extracts. There is rarely any "right" or "wrong" answer. Your opinions and the way you express them are what counts. Often you get ideas from what other people say, so remember that it is important to listen as well as to speak.

The reading, talking and activities in *Cliffhangers* should all be enjoyable, so have fun and Good Reading!

1 The Turbulent Term of Tyke Tiler

by Gene Kemp

Gene Kemp was brought up in a village in the Midlands of England. She was the youngest child of five and enjoyed a happy childhood with little money, a lot of books, several cats and a well in the garden. She studied English at Exeter University and is now married with three children and lives in Exeter. She likes reading, archaeology, gardening and keeping animals. At various times she has kept dogs, cats, mice, gerbils, hamsters, guinea pigs, grass-snakes, fish and budgerigars.

* * * * * * * * * * * *

Tyke Tiler, in the final year at primary school, is always in trouble. Most of the trouble is caused by Tyke's friend, Danny, but he has a face like an angel so Tyke usually gets the blame. At the moment Tyke is panicking about a ten-pound note which Danny has stolen from a teacher's purse, and which at any moment may be traced to them. They go into the school assembly. ...

We started to sing the hymn.

> Father, hear the prayer we offer,
> Not for ease that prayer shall be,
> But for strength that we may ever
> Live our lives courageously.

That's what I needed. Strength.

Danny brought a mouse out of his pocket. Fatty, his black and white piebald. The Head was saying. "God, I shall be very busy today. ... "

Danny placed the mouse in the middle of Linda Stoatway's yellow hair, waving in front of him.

" ... I may forget thee, but do not thou forget me."

Linda Stoatway let out a scream and shot forward, trying to pull out the mouse and her hair as well. She fell over a third-year girl in front of her who toppled on to the boy in front. It's a small hall and there isn't much room. Like ninepins a whole line of children fell forward in it. The one in the front row crashed into Champers at the piano. There was a horrible loud chord – or dischord – and in the confusion, Fatty could be seen heading for the side where the Staff stand. Mrs Somers seemed to be his target. She screeched a high shrill shriek, and climbed the two lowest rungs of the wall bars. Mr Merchant, our teacher, spotted Fatty and did

a flying tackle, landing at Mrs Somers's feet. But Fatty had already moved on, travelling at tremendous speed towards the platform, pursued by several children who all thought they were good mouse-catchers. Very nippily, Chief Sir ran down the steps, picked up Fatty, and mounted the platform again. He looked round the hall. Children crept back to their places. He stood there, not saying a word, until it seemed that something would burst in that hall. No one moved. He stroked Fatty, who looked quite happy sitting there in his hand.

Then he said in a voice like a laser beam:

"I should like the owner of this little fellow to come to my room at playtime."

We walked back to the classroom without a word.

First lesson was Maths. I'd made a duodecahedron which I was going to paint silver and hang up as a mobile. It was a peaceful lesson. Danny was with another group at the other

side of the room, so I couldn't talk to him, and I didn't want to. I just wanted to lie low and keep out of trouble if I could. And it was nice painting my duodecahedron. When Mrs Bennet, the secretary, came in to tell me to go to the Headmaster's office, I'd nearly forgotten everything else. It soon came back, though.

Pitthead called out: "Tyke's got nuthin' to do with it. It was Danny's mouse."

"Get on with your work, Ian."

It was worse than going to the dentist's, more like riding in the tumbrils to the guillotine. Several hours went by as I walked to the office very slowly and carefully, but I reached the door much too soon. I stared at it for a long time, then knocked slowly.

The Headmaster wrote something on a sheet of paper while I stood in front of his desk. I wondered what would happen if I ran out of the room. At last, he looked up. Then he took the ten-pound note out of his pocket and held it towards me.

"Have you seen this before?"

* * * * * * * * * * * *

A. Talking about the story

1. When Danny lets the mouse loose, there is chaos in the school hall. Find all the words and phrases in the passage which show that people are moving quickly and making a lot of noise, and that there is a good deal of confusion.

2. After the confusion, the Head speaks in a voice "like a laser beam". Read his line in the sort of voice you think this means.
   Why does Tyke compare his voice to a laser beam?

3. The real author of this book is a woman called Gene Kemp, but she writes it as though it is Tyke who is telling the story. This is called "Writing in the First Person". What other books do you know that are written in the first person? Do you like this style of writing?
   Why do you think she writes the book in the first person?
   If you read *The Turbulent Term of Tyke Tiler*, you will find that Gene Kemp had a *very* strong reason for making Tyke tell the story, and you will be surprised by it. (Don't tell anyone if you already know.)

B. Talking around the story

1. What do you think the Head will do to Danny and Tyke?
   What would you do if you were the Head?
   What would you do if you were Tyke?

2. Tyke refers to three people by their nicknames. Can you spot the nicknames?
   What do you think the real names might be?
   Why do people use nicknames?
   Do you have any good nicknames for friends or family?
   What are they?

C. Activity: group discussion

You are going to have a group discussion on the subject of "Punishments at School".

With your teacher, go over the rules for group discussions. Work in groups of about eight. You will need to appoint a group leader who will take notes and report back.

Discuss the sorts of punishments that are used at your school. Think of other punishments that could be used instead. Work out among you which punishments you think are the most effective, and which you think serve no purpose. You must have reasons to support all the points you make.

You should end up with two lists. One should be a list of "useful" punishments and the reasons why you think they are useful. The other should be a list of "useless" punishments and the reasons why you think they are useless.

The leaders of each group can then report back to the whole class.

2 Underground to Canada

by Barbara Smucker

Barbara Smucker is an American who now lives in Canada. She wrote her first ever book with a friend when she was still at school. "We decided to bury it," she says, "so it would always be a secret!" After school she trained as a teacher, but she could not keep order in the classroom, so she gave up and went to work on a newspaper instead. Then she began writing novels again. She enjoys writing about history, but tries to make the characters seem as real as if they were alive today.

* * * * * * * * * * *

Julilly and Liza are slaves on a cotton plantation in the Deep South of the USA. They are very cruelly treated by the overseer, and long to escape. One day a man called Mr Ross comes to the plantation pretending to be a bird-watcher; but really he is a representative of the "Underground Railway", an organisation for helping slaves escape to the free country of Canada, far away in the north. Mr Ross arranges to meet Julilly, Liza and two of the men slaves, Adam and Lester, to help them start their escape. They meet late at night in the woods behind the plantation. . . .

"You will start at midnight," he said. "Then everyone will be asleep. I have given Lester a watch so that he will know when the time comes. Make it to the swamp just ahead and wade through the low water in your bare feet. This will kill the scent of tracks. Bloodhounds lose their scent in water."

He paused again for a brief moment to listen.

"Tonight you will follow the great Mississippi River north. It will guide your feet and the North Star above will guide your eyes."

He began talking more quickly. The moon was nearing the height of its climb across the sky.

"By all means, stay together. Lester will be your guide. Trust him. I have given him many directions. You will travel by night and sleep by day. When you cross the border into Tennessee, I will be there. Pretend you don't know me and don't be astonished at my face, for my beard will be shaved."

He stopped talking and handed each of them two dollar bills, a knife and some cold meat and bread. To Julilly and Liza he gave a pair of pants and a shirt.

"Change these after you cross the swamp," he said. "Let your old clothes float on the water. The slave hunters might think you have drowned. Lester has scissors to clip your hair short."

He shook hands with each of them, clasping them tightly.

"Now I must go back to the Big House. Tomorrow I leave for another mission in Columbus, Mississippi. Bless you."

He walked swiftly away from them through the shadow-filled forest.

"Massa Ross is a good man." Julilly spoke for all of them.

When they could no longer hear his footsteps, Julilly, Liza and Adam turned to Lester.

"Put everything he gave you in your crocker sack and fasten it to your back," he said. There was no expression on Lester's face, but Julilly saw fear and excitement in his eyes.

He looked at the watch, round and smooth in his hand. It was time to go.

"No one is huntin' for us tonight," Lester said. "We got to cover a lot of ground."

Julilly glanced at Liza. Her head was down, and her back was bent, which meant that it was already hurting her.

"I'm gonna walk by Liza," Julilly stated firmly. "We've agreed to help each other."

Julilly grabbed a drooping willow branch with one hand to keep her steady; with the other hand she held Liza's arm, guiding the bent girl along beside her.

Julilly was grateful for the soft moonlight. It illumined dead branches jutting from the water and water-knees protruding from the tall swamp cypress.

Twice she felt the shell of a turtle slip under her feet.

"I hope those old alligators and water-moccasins are sleepin' tonight like they are dead," Julilly whispered to Liza.

"Don't put your mind on things such as that," Liza whispered back. "And don't forget, no bloodhound can smell our scent through this ol' swamp water."

At last the ground became more solid. Then it was dry again. Now was the time for Julilly and Liza to change into their boys' clothes and throw the worn tow shirts on top of the swamp water. Lester quickly clipped their hair with scissors from his knapsack.

There was no time at all to giggle over their changed appearance. Lester was impatient to go on. Already they could hear the flow of the great Mississippi River.

* * * *

The escaping slaves trudge along the river banks all night long. Then at dawn they settle down to sleep, taking it in turns to keep guard. When it is Julilly's turn she sits for a while enjoying her new-found freedom. . . .

A mockingbird sailed through the sky, then perched above her and sang its own clear song. A gentle deer walked serenely to the river's edge and dipped its head for a long drink.

It was peaceful to sit so quiet. But it didn't last. The deer jerked its head upright. It listened and then ran back among the trees. The mockingbird chirped a mixed-up song of many birds, then sped away.

Julilly sat tense. Softly at first and then louder came the

cry of baying dogs. Bloodhounds! Somehow their scent had
been found and they or other slaves like them were being
followed. Lester heard too. He shook Adam. Julilly called
Liza.

"Pack everything in your bags." Lester spoke quickly.
"Roll up your pants, and we'll walk north, straight through
the middle of this stream. It will kill our scent."

* * * * * * * * * * * *

A. Talking about the story

1. Look at the second episode from the book.
   There are two different moods created in this section.
   What are they?
   At what point does the mood change? How does the author
   bring about the change of mood?

2. Massa Ross gave the slaves instructions about how to
   organise their escape — what to do and where to go.
   Your teacher will choose someone to note the main points
   of this escape plan *in the right order* on the blackboard.
   The rest of the class should study the section of the passage,
   from the beginning to "Lester has scissors to clip your hair
   short". They should tell the blackboard-writer what to
   write.

B. Talking around the story

1. Why do you think people wanted to keep slaves?
   Nowadays, slavery is regarded as very wrong. Why is this?

2. The "Underground Railway" to Canada was a famous slave
   escape route. There are many other sorts of captivity, from
   which people have tried to escape. Tell the class of any
   famous escape stories that you know.

C. Activity: cliffhangers

Work in groups of about four.

You are going to make up an escape story of your own, around the group. Each person will tell the story for a while, making it as exciting as possible, and ending with the hero in a very difficult or dangerous situation. The next person must carry on where the first has left off. He must make the hero escape from the situation he is in, and then continue the story, until the hero is in another difficult or dangerous plight. The third person carries on the story in the same way, and so on. Try to go round the group at least twice.

You can invent your own hero if you like, or you can choose one of these:

> Edward Perry, *gentleman burglar*
> Ron Redfoot, *American secret agent*
> Aileen Seaweed, *glamorous spy*
> Ishbel Bernard, *French Resistance worker*
> Skip Castro, *Mexican bandit.*

3 The Cartoonist
by Betsy Byars

Betsy Byars is an American and lives in West Virginia. She has been writing books for young readers ever since her own children started reading. She does her writing in the winter months, because her husband's hobby is hang-gliding and their summers are filled with work on a sailplane and driving a ten-metre trailer around to competitions. She says, "My books usually begin with something that really happened, a newspaper story or an event from my children's lives." She spends a year writing a book, but then spends another year thinking about it and improving it.

* * * * * * * * * * * *

Alfie lives with his mother, grandfather (Pap) and sister Alma in a small rickety house in an American city. He also has an elder brother, Bubba, who is rather a tearaway, but Bubba is married now, and has moved to another town. Alfie's mother misses Bubba, whom she thinks is good fun. She doesn't understand Alfie. He likes to spend his time in the attic, where he draws endless cartoons. It's quiet up there and he can be alone. Then one day Alma tells Alfie that Bubba and his wife are coming back to live with them.

Suddenly Alfie's mind turned to the crooked house – the two bedrooms, the living-room, the bathroom, the kitchen.

That's all there was, he thought. The sofa in the living-room didn't even make into a bed.

"But where are they going to sleep?" Alfie asked, following her. He went over the sleeping arrangements. He and Pap shared one bedroom, Alma and his mother, the other. There was no room for Bubba and Maureen. His hopes rose. "There's nowhere for them to sleep!"

"Mom's going to fix up the attic."

For a moment he felt as if he had been hit over the head with a hammer. He was paralysed.

"The attic?" he muttered.

"Yeah, she's got it all planned. She's getting a window from Mr Wilkins, and she's talking Pap into cutting a hole in the eaves and installing it. Then she's getting a double bed from Hill's Used Furniture and *my* dressing table and – "

"But the attic belongs to me." He stammered for the first time since he was three. His knees felt weak. In his mind the attic wavered like a desert mirage.

He had once watched an old apartment building on High Street being demolished. A huge ball had pounded into the walls, and they had crumbled. As the dust settled, Alfie could see pieces of people's lives shimmering in the air – the old faded wallpapers they had chosen, the linoleum they had walked on. An old curtain had flapped from a third-storey window. Finally everything had sunk into a mound of dust. His attic crumbled now in the same way, his cartoons fluttering down through the dusty air like autumn leaves.

"The attic *used* to be yours," Alma corrected.

"No, it's *mine*."

"As soon as I get home with the cleaning stuff, Mom's going to start on it, and tomorrow – if she can talk Pap into it – the window will be installed, and by noon it'll be Bubba's bedroom."

"Mom wouldn't do that to me."

"Alfie, Mom would do anything for Bubba. Haven't you learned that by now?"

"They're not taking my attic." His face looked so pale and strained that Alma shifted her groceries to reach out and touch him.

"Hey, it's not the end of the world," she said. . . .

"They're not going to take my attic."

She shook his shoulder gently. "Hey, look, it's – "

He glanced at her without seeing her. "Nobody's going to take my attic." Twisting away from her hand, he turned and began to run for home.

"Wait, Alfie," Alma called. "Wait!" Clutching the groceries, she hurried after him.

As he ran past the Hunters' house, his mother stuck her head out the door and called to him. "Alfie!" He didn't look at her. "Alfie, stop. Wait a minute! I've got some wonderful news."

Alfie kept running. He took the steps in one bound, went down on his knees, got up, lunged for the screen door, pulled himself up by the knob, and entered. It was all one long awkward motion.

His mother started after him and called back to Mrs Hunter, "I'll send Alfie and Pap over for the chest of drawers after supper." She paused to adjust her thong sandal. "And Bubba and Maureen will take real good care of it."

Alfie plunged across the living-room. He grabbed the ladder as a man being swept away in a flood grabs for a tree. He swayed in the current.

Pap loomed up in the kitchen doorway, filling it. He held a coffee mug in one hand, a jelly doughnut in the other. "Did you hear the news?" He paused to lick some jelly from the side of his thumb.

Alfie started up the ladder. He felt the pull of gravity for the first time in his life. His feet were lead. His pants were nailed to the floor. He would never reach the attic.

"Bubba's coming home," Pap said.

Alfie struggled for the next rung of the ladder. He swayed with the unseen current. He struck his head on the wall.

"Bubba *and* Maureen."

Alfie reached up with one shaking hand. He pushed at the trapdoor. It was heavy. Usually it sprang open at his touch. Now it wouldn't budge. He went up another rung of the ladder. He put his head to it. Goat-like, he began to shove the door open.

"I don't mind him coming so much as I do her," Pap said, sitting on the sofa. "I don't know why Bubba had to marry a girl that pops gum all the time." He licked his thumb again. "And she'll leave it anywhere. One time I found a big wad of bubble gum in my tooth-glass. It scared me. I thought my teeth had shrivelled."

Heaving as if he had climbed a tall mountain instead of a ladder, Alfie pulled himself into the attic. He crawled forward. He let the trapdoor shut behind him. The slam was like a cannon firing, the first shot of a long and difficult war.

"Alfie!"

He lay stretched out on the dusty attic floor, completely spent. Faintly he heard his mother call him as she came in the front door.

"Alfie, don't go up in the attic. I want to talk to you. I've got some great news."

"I done told him the great news," Pap said from the sofa.

"And guess what, Pap? Mrs Hunter's got a chest she's going to let me use. She just covered it with contact paper – red and orange pansies – and it's going to really brighten up the attic. I'm getting so excited. Look at me, Pap. My hands are trembling."

In the attic Alfie's hands were trembling too. He got slowly to his knees.

When he had first started doing his cartoons in the attic, he had worked out a way of locking the trapdoor so nobody could come up and catch him unaware. Now he took the board and slipped it over the trapdoor and under the floorboards on either side.

"Alfie, what are you doing up there?" his mother called. "Come on down. I want to talk to you." She said to Pap, "Is there any coffee left?" She went into the kitchen.

On his knees Alfie stared blankly at the trapdoor. The board was in place now. No one could open it.

* * * * * * * * * * * * *

A. Talking about the story

1. What kind of person do you think Alfie's mother is? Find clues in the passage to support your view.

2. "In his mind the attic wavered like a desert mirage." What is a mirage? Why is this a good comparison?
   Find four or five comparisons like this in the passage. Discuss how they help you picture what is happening in your mind.

B. Talking around the story

1. Alma says to Alfie, "Hey, it's not the end of the world." She means that although things seem very bad at the time, Alfie will get over them sooner or later.
   Do you think this is true? Can you think of times when you have thought that something was "the end of the world"? Give examples to support your view.

2. Alfie likes drawing his own cartoons.
   What is the difference between a cartoon and an ordinary picture?
   What cartoon characters do you know?
   Why do people enjoy cartoons?
   Which is your favourite, and why?

C. Activity: commentary

Work in pairs. You should each have a comic strip in front of you. Study it carefully, making sure that you understand what is happening in each of the pictures.

Then take turns to give a commentary on your comic strip to your partner. You should try to commentate as though the events in the pictures are happening as you speak, and you should make the story as exciting and interesting as you can. If someone talks in the comic strip, you should say who it is, and give the words they say. If someone moves, you should try to convey the way they move.

The one who is listening should ask questions wherever the commentary is not clear.

4 Grinny
by Nicholas Fisk

Nicholas Fisk has been an actor, jazz musician, illustrator, photographer, copywriter, publisher and writer. Nowadays he concentrates mainly on writing, particularly science fiction books for young people. He believes that almost any imaginable possibility may become a reality within the lifetime of someone who is young now. His interests include snorkelling, cars, music, old microscopes, swimming in his own pool (heated by a solar heater he designed) and photography.

* * * * * * * * * * * *

This story is told in the form of a diary, written by Timothy Carpenter, aged eleven. It begins in mid-January. . . .

Jan. 14

Astonishing news! I had come back from Mac's house and had just been shouted at as usual by Mum (TAKE YOUR BOOTS OFF) when I heard the station taxi grinding up the drive and soon after, our bell being rung. I was still in the porch so I opened the door and *there she was*, all five feet one of her, with two gi-normous trunks. I did not know what to say, but she said, "I am your Great Aunt Emma. You must be Tim," and I mumbled something about calling Mother, but Mum had heard the bell go and came hurtling along the corridor shouting, "If it's the Guides, it must wait till Tuesday and if it's Mac, tell him to TAKE HIS BOOTS OFF." When she goes to heaven, she will say this to all the archangels.

I said, "It's Great Aunt Emma, Mum, were you expecting –?" but she simply said, "Most amusing, you *witty* lad!" in her Wednesday matinee voice and went belting past on her way to the kitchen. Then she caught a glimpse of Aunt Emma and stopped in her tracks and came to the doorway. "*Who?*" she said. "Great Aunt *who?*" I could see she was completely foxed and had never heard of GAE, as I will henceforth refer to Great Aunt Emma, as she is bound to figure largely in these pages from now on.

GAE said, "You remember me, Millie!" but Mum could only see a vague shape and replied, "Oh dear, I am afraid I don't quite remember – " Then I switched on the porch light and Mum could see GAE properly. GAE leaned forward and said again, "You remember me, Millie!" and this time the penny dropped and Mum cried out, "Great Aunt Emma! Oh do come in, you must be freezing. Tim, help with the luggage!"

So we got her inside and she is rather a queer old party. Very short, with a hat with a veil, and gloves, and a way of smiling vaguely. Her teeth are very good (false?) and she is very neat. Her shoes hardly have creases in them over the instep, as if she never walked, yet she is quite spry considering her age and soon she and Mum were chattering away about the journey and so on. At first Mum didn't seem quite with the situation, I could tell she was faking a lot, but she is such a good faker (unlike Father) that only an outsider could have told that she was a bit baffled by GAE. Anyhow, this soon passed, I saw her (Mum) wipe the back of her hand across her brow which is always a sign that her mind is now made up and Into Action! After another few minutes you could have sworn that Mum had been expecting GAE for the last fortnight, that the bed was aired and so on. She is very good at that sort of thing.

* * * *

As the weeks go by, Timothy and his sister Beth notice that Great Aunt Emma is rather strange. She doesn't seem to feel the cold, she is frightened of electricity, she never speaks about her past life, and she is *always* asking questions. They nickname her Grinny because of her perpetual, rather unpleasant grin.

Beth particularly becomes frightened of her. And then Timothy finds out why. . . .

Feb. 9

This is not easy to write. I know I send up Beth all the time and make jokes about WAW* and so on and she is after all only a seven-year-old (but soon to be eight) – but she is

---

*Women Always Win (a family joke)

nothing like such a fool as I like to make her out to be and if she is a liar, she is doing it very well – even crying with the lying. I don't know what to make of it.

She was sitting in her room and refusing to come down. Eventually Mum sent me up to tell Beth that dinner was nearly on the table and that she really must come down. I crashed into Beth's room and said, "Oh, come on, Beth, it's dinner time and I've had to come all the way upstairs," etc., etc. She just burst into tears and said she wasn't coming down, she refused to come down, leave me alone and so on.

She looked so awful that I didn't start on her in the usual way but tried to be nice – what's wrong, did something happen at school, aren't you well. She said, "No, no, it's her – Grinny! It's Grinny!" Anyhow, Mum was standing at the foot of the stairs yelling for us to come down so I pulled her (Beth) to her feet and said, "Will you tell me after?" and she replied, "Yes, but only if you promise!" Which means of course promise not to tell anyone else.

She was quiet and white at dinner but I don't think any-one took much notice as there were two men from the site, a stonemason and a photographer, having a meal with us and they and Father kept talking shop at the top of their voices all the time. Beth ate as much as usual. But as soon as the meal was over and we had cleared the dishes, she tugged at my arm and made me go back with her to her room.

She said, "I've been longing to tell someone, but they'll only laugh. Will you laugh?" I said no. She said, "Do you think I am just a stupid little girl or don't you? Because I'm not." She started crying again so I gave her the old hug and kiss treatment, which I don't often do, so when I do do it it works all the better (*do do it it* is like a word puzzle). It worked now – she stopped crying, stared me straight in the face and said –

"*Grinny's not real.*"

I said, "Oh." I was disappointed in her for being so childish, actually.

She said, "Yes, I knew you would take it like that, you just think I'm stupid, but I am not. *Grinny is not real*, she's not a real person at all."

It went on like this for a little while, then I said, "Tell me exactly and precisely what you are talking about and no messing about and above all do not cry."

She said, "You remember the day she fell down on the ice and hurt herself?" I said yes. "Well, I was the first one there, I was there just about a second after she did it, she was still lying on the ground and I was there beside her. And I saw something you will never believe, never!"

I said what was it and I would try to believe her.

She said, "Something horrible, it was *horrible*! I saw her wrist actually broken and the bone sticking out!"

I replied, "That's impossible. Do be reasonable, she was perfectly all right quite soon after. If you break your wrist it is very serious, it takes weeks or months to mend. Particularly if you are old. And it is very painful, agony, in fact. So you just couldn't have seen it, Beth, you only thought you saw it because you have a good imagination."

Beth said, "I haven't got a good imagination, Penny writes much better essays than I do and so does Sue. I saw it, I saw it, I saw it!"

So I made her tell me just what it was she saw. She started off by repeating that I would never believe her and so on, but in the end it came down to this – I am choosing my words very carefully so as not to distort what she said –

"She was lying on the ground in a heap. She was not groaning or moaning, just lying there and kicking her legs, trying to get up. I went close to her and got hold of her elbow so that I could help pull her up. She did not say anything to me, like "Help me" or "My wrist hurts" – she just tried to get up. When I seized her elbow, I saw her wrist. The hand was dangling. The wrist was so badly broken that the skin was all cut open in a gash and the bones were showing."

I told Beth I understood all this, but she seemed unwilling to go on. She looked at me and wailed, "Oh, it's no good, you'll never believe me!" but I made her go on. She said:

"The skin was gashed open but there was no blood. The bones stuck out but they were not made of real bone – they were made of shiny steel!"

A. Talking about the story

1. What do you think Grinny is?
   What parts of the story make you think this?

2. This story is written as a diary. There are many features of
   the writing style which show us that it is a diary, which
   was written in haste and in a casual way. Look through the
   passage again and pick out as many words and phrases as
   possible which make it seem to you like a diary.

B. Talking around the story

1. Timothy refers to a joke he and his father share that "Women
   Always Win".
   Many men think that women always get the best of things.
   Why is this?
   Many women think that men always have things their own
   way. Why is this?
   What do you think? Why?

2. *Grinny* is a science fiction book.
   What does "science fiction" mean?
   Do you like science fiction? Why, or why not?
   It is a very popular type of fiction. Why do you think so
   many people like it so much?

C. Activity: Animal, Vegetable or Mineral?

This is a panel game. Work in groups of about five.
All but one of you should sit in a row as the panel. The other
one is the challenger.
The challenger thinks of something. It can be anything from
"the King of Spain" to "a plate of chips". He doesn't tell the
panel what it is, only whether it is Animal, Vegetable, or

Mineral, or a combination of any of these. He must also say how many words it consists of, and whether any of them are the definite article ("the") or the indefinite article ("a" or "an").

> Animal — any animal, dead or alive, or something made from part of an animal (e.g. leather, which is from a cow).
>
> Vegetable — any plant, dead or alive, or something made from part of a plant (e.g. paper, which is made from wood).
>
> Mineral — something that has never been alive (like stone, or sand, or metal) or something made from minerals (like glass or a tin box).

The King of Spain would just be "Animal". It is four words, and the first is the definite article. A plate of chips would be "Mineral" (the plate) and "Vegetable" (the chips). It is four words and the first is an indefinite article.

If you're not absolutely sure what something is made of, you will have to go and whisper to your teacher, who will probably know.

The panel has thirty questions with which to guess the object. The challenger can only answer "yes", "no" or "I don't know". If the panel cannot guess what the object is in thirty questions, the challenger has won.

Take it in turns to be the challenger.

Other Good Reads

If you enjoyed *The Eighteenth Emergency*, watch out for other books by Betsy Byars, like *The Pinballs** (Puffin). This one is about three children, all misfits, who turn up at the same foster home. It looks as though Carlie is too aggressive, Thomas J. is too timid, and Harvey is too unhappy for them ever to get along together, but plenty happens before the end of the book.

In *Underground to Canada*, you met some black slaves in the Southern States of the USA, but even when slavery ended, life for the black people there was not easy. *Roll of Thunder, Hear My Cry*** by Mildred D. Taylor (Puffin) is a dramatic and moving story about a black American family in the 1930's, and the problems they have to face.

*The Machine Gunners*** by Robert Westall (Puffin) is set during the Second World War in an industrial town in the North of England. It is a gripping, often violent story about a group of children who find a machine gun on the tail of a shot-down German plane, and decide to use it to help fight the war themselves. This is a very exciting book, but it's for people with strong stomachs only!

Another exciting story of the Second World War is *Puddles in the Lane*** by Alan Parker (Star books). It's about a family from the slums of London, who are caught up in the terrible events of the Blitz and then evacuated to the countryside. But even far from the bombing their lives continue to be exciting and eventful.

Another dramatic story is *I am David*** by Anna Holm (Puffin). In the first pages, its young hero, David, escapes from a terrible prison camp where he has been held since he was a baby. He has to make his way across Europe, ignorant of the ways of the world, and pursued by the mysterious "Them", in the hope of finding his home and family.

If you're looking for a straightforward modern thriller, you might try *Chips and the Crossword Gang** by Roy Brown (Granada). Chips, the son of a policeman, takes on a newspaper round to earn some extra money, and finds himself on the trail of a gang of thieves. Good solid adventurous stuff.

A couple of funny, very easy and quick reads are *Vlad the Drac** by Ann Jungman (Dragon books) and *The Twits** by Roald Dahl (Puffin). *Vlad the Drac* is a very unusual vampire, who faints at the sight of blood! He is found in the snows of Transylvania by Paul and Judy, who smuggle him home and keep him hidden in their bedrooms. Vlad, however, frequently escapes and causes all sorts of trouble. Trouble is also the theme of *The Twits*. Mr and Mrs Twit are a thoroughly horrible couple who delight in playing nasty tricks on each other. The episodes of the glass eye in the mug of beer, the frog in the bed, and the wormy spaghetti are just the beginning of their nastiness!

Finally, one of the best books for people in their last year at Primary School — *Gowie Corby Plays Chicken** (Puffin). By Gene Kemp, who wrote *Tyke Tiler*, this is the story of a truly *awful* boy, his quarrels with his classmates, his dreadful behaviour at school, his obsession with horror story characters, and his pet rat, Boris. It is also a hilariously funny and exciting story. Highly recommended.

5 Cue for Treason
by Geoffrey Trease

Geoffrey Trease was born in 1909 in Nottingham. He has always loved history and the theatre, and *Cue for Treason* combines both of these. Since leaving University in mid-course to seek his fortune as a writer, he has produced scores of plays, poems and novels for young people and adults.

* * * * * * * * * * * *

This book is set in Elizabethan England, about four hundred years ago. Peter Brownrigg, a young boy from Cumberland, is in trouble. He has thrown a rock at a local nobleman, Sir Philip Morton, and Sir Philip is after him, intent on revenge. Knowing that the penalty for his crime could be hanging, or having his nose slit or his ears cropped, Peter runs away from home across the mountains. Eventually he arrives in the market town of Penrith, where he stops for a rest. Some travelling actors are about to perform a play in an inn-yard, so Peter decides to go and watch.

By now the inn-yard was fairly crowded, and there were people filling the upper galleries all round, which led to the bedrooms. The players had rigged up a platform on trestles at one end of the yard, and we all moved round, some of us with our stools, but most of the people standing. I'd finished my mutton and licked my greasy fingers when suddenly I got a shock which turned the good food over inside me.

Sir Philip Morton was coming through the archway into the yard.

He paused to give his penny to the man, and I saw his lean face sideways, with the little golden beard springing from the cruel under-lip, and the blue eyes so cold and insolent.

"And we'll have stools, my man, on the stage. What? No stools allowed on the stage? Absurd! Too poky, I suppose. Very well." He turned and waved a gloved hand towards my corner of the yard. "Put me two over there, then."

I thought I was done for.

There was only the one archway leading from the yard, and Sir Philip stood there, ordering wine. I could not pass him, but if I stayed where I was he would come and sit down almost beside me.

I looked round like a fox trapped on a ledge. Then I thought of the galleries.

A staircase rose close behind me. If I went up there I might find some other way out, or at any rate I might be able to lie hidden in some room till the play was over.

Without wasting any more time, I slipped off my stool and up that staircase. The gallery was already crowded with people, ready settled to see the play. One way they were so thickly packed that I couldn't push quickly through without starting an uproar, which was the last thing I wanted to do. The other way there weren't so many. Just then I heard Sir Philip's voice on the stairs:

"We should see better up here, Roger, and we shouldn't get our toes trodden on by these clodhopping shepherds."

"Just as you like, Phil."

I didn't wait for more. There was a curtained doorway at the end of the gallery, and I made for it, stumbling over people's heels and mumbling my apologies.

"Hey! you there, *boy*!"

That was Sir Philip's voice from the top of the stairs. He'd seen me. I rushed on, flung out my hand to part the curtain.

"Stop that boy!" he shouted.

I heard the people behind me cursing heartily at being disturbed when the play was about to begin. I hurled myself through the curtain, round the corner of a dark landing, and down a staircase. I found myself in the midst of a crowd of feverishly excited people – I was in the actors' dressing-room.

A boy was being helped into an immense hooped skirt, the fat man was grumbling because his armour would not meet round the back, a tall, gloomy young man was reciting lines to himself in a thin, birdlike voice. . . . This much I had time to take in before the fat man bellowed at me:

"Who are you? What do you want? Get out of here! We're ready to go on, and I *will* not have outsiders behind the scene. Vanish, before I rend you limb from limb!"

He was a terrifying figure. I ducked under his arm, getting no more than a glancing clout which made my head sing, and rushed round a corner into another passage. Behind me I heard him roaring:

"What? More intruders! Out with you, sir! I don't care
if you're Sir – "

"This gentleman with me is a magistrate," Sir Philip cut
in very icily.

I heard this all plainly, for the very good reason that I
was trapped in the passage outside. There were only two
doors leading from it, and they were both locked. The passage
seemed to be a dumping-ground for stage properties and
costumes.

I thought wildly for a moment of disguising myself in one
of these costumes – a woman's spreading skirts would have
been the best concealment – but I realised that the actors
would give me away at once.

"My friend is a magistrate," Sir Philip was saying, "and you'll realise that, if he likes, he can forbid your play altogether and ruin your tour in this part of the country. So you'd better be civil."

"What do you want, sir?" the fat man growled. I could tell he was bottling up his fury with great difficulty.

You mustn't think that I stood still, listening to their talk and doing nothing. The whole thing took only a few seconds, and I wasted none of them.

There was a big chest among the actors' properties; I suppose it was used for storing costumes when they moved from place to place. It was long, narrow, and deep. Also, it was empty and unlocked.

It was a desperate chance, but the only one. I hopped inside and pulled down the lid. As I did so I heard a trumpet sound, and a great burst of stamping and clapping in the distance. The fat man's voice sounded despairing:

"But, gentlemen, the play's just beginning!"

"Carry on with your play; we don't mind," said Sir Philip. "But we insist on searching these rooms."

* * * * * * * * * * * *

A. Talking about the story

1. In this passage, the author describes how and where a play was acted in Elizabethan times. Find as many differences as you can between this and a play performed in a theatre today.

2. What kind of character do you think Sir Philip Morton is? Find evidence in the passage to support your view.

B. Talking around the story

1. Have you ever been to see, or appeared in, a play? If so,
   what was the play?
   Did you enjoy it? Why, or why not?
   How does going to a play compare with going to a film?

2. The boy in the story thinks of disguising himself to escape
   his pursuers. On what other occasions might people want
   to disguise themselves?
   In what different ways can people disguise themselves?
   If teachers in your school wanted to disguise themselves,
   in what ways would you suggest they should go about it?

C. Activity: giving a prepared talk

Everyone should have prepared a talk, lasting about three
minutes, on a historical character. These should now be given
to the rest of the class.

As you listen to other people's talks, try to notice what makes
them good or bad, interesting or boring.

6 Nothing To Be Afraid Of

by Jan Mark

Jan Mark's mother taught her to read when she was three, and she's been a compulsive reader ever since. Her writing career started early too, when she won a *Daily Mirror* short story competition at the age of fifteen. As a teacher in Kent, she wrote plays – "comedies with lots of fights". Now she lives in a Norfolk village with her husband, son and daughter, and keeps up her hobbies: reading, pottery, rescuing derelict cats and watching aircraft.

* * * * * * * * * * * *

This is a collection of short stories. The first one is about Anthea, who has been asked to look after a little boy called Robin. He is four years old and *terribly* boring: he never speaks, and seems to have no interest in anything except his cuddly toy, Doggy. Anthea takes Robin for a walk in the local park, and as they trudge around the paths she becomes more bored than ever. She is very keen to make Robin react to something – anything!

On the first circuit Robin stumped glumly beside Anthea in front of the bushes. The second time round she felt a very faint tug at her hand. Robin wanted to go his own way.

This called for a celebration. Robin could think. Anthea crouched down on the path until they were at the same level.

"You want to walk round the back of the bushes, Robin?"

"Yiss," said Robin.

Robin could *talk*.

"All right, but listen." She lowered her voice to a whisper. "You must be very careful. That path is called Leopard Walk. Do you know what a leopard is?"

"Yiss."

"There are two leopards down there. They live in the bushes. One is a good leopard and the other's a bad leopard. The good leopard has black spots. The bad leopard has red spots. If you see the bad leopard you must say, 'Die leopard die or I'll kick you in the eye', and run like anything. Do you understand?"

Robin tugged again.

"Oh no," said Anthea. "I'm going *this* way. If you want to go down Leopard Walk, you'll have to go on your own. I'll meet you at the other end. Remember, if it's got red spots, run like mad."

Robin trotted away. The bushes were just high enough to hide him, but Anthea could see the bobble on his hat doddering along. Suddenly the bobble gathered speed and Anthea had to run to reach the end of the bushes first.

"Did you see the bad leopard?"

"No," said Robin, but he didn't look too sure.

"Why were you running, then?"

"I just wanted to."

"You've dropped Doggy," said Anthea. Doggy lay on the path with his legs in the air, halfway down Leopard Walk.

"You get him," said Robin.

35 "No, *you* get him," said Anthea. "I'll wait here." Robin moved off, reluctantly. She waited until he had recovered Doggy and then shouted, "I can see the bad leopard in the bushes!" Robin raced back to safety. "Did you say, 'Die leopard die or I'll kick you in the eye'?" Anthea demanded.

40 "No," Robin said, guiltily.

"Then he'll *kill* us," said Anthea. "Come on, run. We've got to get to that tree. He can't hurt us once we're under that tree."

They stopped running under the twisted boughs of a
45 weeping ash. "This is a python tree," said Anthea. "Look, you can see the python wound round the trunk."

"What's a python?" said Robin, backing off.

"Oh, it's just a great big snake that squeezes people to death," said Anthea. "A python could easily eat a leopard.
50 That's why leopards won't walk under this tree, you see, Robin."

Robin looked up. "Could it eat us?"

"Yes, but it won't if we walk on our heels." They walked on their heels to the next corner.
55 "Are there leopards down there?"

"No, but we must never go down there anyway. That's Poison Alley. All the trees are poisonous. They drip poison. If one bit of poison fell on your head, you'd die."

"I've got my hat on," said Robin, touching the bobble to
60 make sure.

"It would burn right through your hat," Anthea assured him. "Right into your brains. *Fzzzzzzz.*"

They by-passed Poison Alley and walked on over the manhole cover that clanked.
65 "What's that?"

"That's the Fever Pit. If anyone lifts that manhole cover, they get a terrible disease. There's this terrible disease down there, Robin, and if the lid comes off, the disease will get out and people will die. I should think there's enough disease down there to kill everybody in this town. It's ever so loose, look."

"Don't lift it! Don't lift it!" Robin screamed, and ran to the shelter for safety.

"Don't go in there," yelled Anthea. "That's where the Greasy Witch lives." Robin bounced out of the shelter as though he were on elastic.

"Where's the Greasy Witch?"

"Oh, you can't see her," said Anthea, "but you can tell

where she is because she smells so horrible. I think she must
be somewhere about. Can't you smell her now?"

Robin sniffed the air and clasped Doggy more tightly.

"And she leaves oily marks wherever she goes. Look, you
can see them on the wall."

Robin looked at the wall. Someone had been very busy,
if not the Greasy Witch. Anthea was glad on the whole that
Robin could not read.

"The smell's getting worse, isn't it, Robin? I think we'd
better go down here and then she won't find us."

"She'll see us."

"No, she won't. She can't see with her eyes because they're
full of grease. She sees with her ears, but I expect they're all
waxy. She's a filthy old witch, really."

They slipped down a secret-looking path that went round
the back of the shelter.

"Is the Greasy Witch down here?" said Robin, fearfully.

"I don't know," said Anthea. "Let's investigate." They
tiptoed round the side of the shelter. The path was damp
and slippery. "Filthy old witch. She's certainly *been* here,"
said Anthea. "I think she's gone now. I'll just have a look."
She craned her neck round the corner of the shelter. There
was a sort of glade in the bushes, and in the middle was a
stand-pipe, with a tap on top. The pipe was lagged with
canvas, like a scaly skin.

"Frightful Corner," said Anthea. Robin put his cautious
head round the edge of the shelter.

"What's that?"

Anthea wondered if it could be a dragon, up on the tip
of its tail and ready to strike, but on the other side of the
bushes was the brick back wall of the King Street Public

Conveniences, and at that moment she heard the unmistak-
able sound of a cistern flushing.

"It's a Lavatory Demon," she said. "Quick! We've got
to get away before the water stops, or he'll have us."

* * * * * * * * * * * *

A. Talking about the story

1. Look for all the names of dangerous places and people
   that Anthea makes up. Which do you think would be most
   frightening to a little child? Why?

2. (a) Do you think Anthea enjoyed her outing with Robin?
       Why do you give that answer?
   (b) Do you think Robin enjoyed the outing?
       Why do you give that answer?

B. Talking around the story

1. People sometimes seem to like being frightened. Think of
   some "entertainments", which are designed to frighten
   people.
   Have you ever enjoyed being frightened in this way?
   Why do you think people like it?

2. Doggy is obviously Robin's favourite toy.
   Do you know any little children who have a favourite toy
   or object which they take with them everywhere? If you
   do, what things have these children chosen?
   Do you remember what you loved best when you were
   little?

C. Activity: summarising

Anthea does not tell her stories in detail. Sometimes it is necessary to give only the main points of a story very briefly. We call this summarising.

Each person should choose one of the Cliffhangers from this book — choose one you have already read. Read it again carefully, and decide in your mind what are the main points of the story.

Take it in turns to summarise your stories to the class. Each summary should be brief — a minute at the most.

Some people will have chosen the same stories. Listen carefully and compare the summaries.

At the end, discuss what makes a good summary. Are some passages easier to summarise than others? Why?

7 Freaky Friday
by Mary Rodgers

Mary Rodgers has many jobs. She is a novelist, a magazine writer, a composer and lyricist, a wife and the mother of five children. She is the daughter of the famous composer, Richard Rodgers. He and Oscar Hammerstein wrote many popular musicals together. Mary says that she wrote *Freaky Friday* "because I wanted both kids and adults to have some fun". The novel has been made into a successful Walt Disney film, and she has also written a sequel to it called *A Billion for Boris*.

* * * * * * * * * * * *

You are not going to believe me, nobody in their right minds could *possibly* believe me, but it's true, really it is!

When I woke up this morning, I found I'd turned into my mother. There I was, in my mother's bed, with my feet reaching all the way to the bottom, and my father sleeping in the other bed. I had on my mother's nightgown, and a ring on my left hand, I mean her left hand, and lumps and pins all over my head.

"I think that must be the rollers," I said to myself, "and if I have my mother's hair, I probably have her face, too."

I decided to take a look at myself in the bathroom mirror. After all, you don't turn into your mother every day of the week; maybe I was imagining it – or dreaming.

Well, I wasn't. What I saw in that mirror was absolutely my mother from top to toe, complete with no braces on the teeth. Now ordinarily, I don't bother to brush too often – it's a big nuisance with all those wires – but my mother's teeth looked like a fun job, and besides, if she was willing to do a terrific thing like turning her body over to me like that, the least I could do was take care of her teeth for *her*. Right? Right.

You see, I had reason to believe that she was responsible for this whole happening. Because last night, we had a sort of an argument about something and I told her one or two things that had been on my mind lately. . . . I can't stand how strict she is. Take food, for instance. Do you know what she makes me eat for breakfast? Cereal, orange juice, toast, an egg, milk, and two Vitamin Cs. She's going to turn me into a blimp. Then for lunch at school, you have one of two choices. You can bring your own bag lunch, with a jelly sandwich or a TV dinner (they're quite good cold) and a Coke, or if you're me, you have to eat the hot meal the school

gives you, which is not hot and I wouldn't give it to a dog. Alpo is better. I know because our dog eats Alpo and I tried some once.

She's also very fussy about the way I keep my room. Her idea of neat isn't the same as mine, and besides, it's my room and I don't see why I can't keep it any way I want. She says it's so messy nobody can clean in there, but if that's true, how come it looks all right when I come home from school? When I asked her that last night, she just sighed.

A few other things we fight about are my hair – she wants me to have it trimmed but I'm not falling for that again (The last time it was "trimmed" they hacked six inches off it!) – and my nails which I bite.

But the biggest thing we fight about is freedom, because I'm old enough to be given more than I'm getting. I'm not allowed to walk home through the park even with a friend, because "New York is a very dangerous place and especially the park". Everybody else's mother lets them, "but I'm not everybody else's mother". You're telling me!

Tomorrow one of my best friends in school who lives in the Village is having a boy-girl party and she won't let me go because the last time that friend had a party they played kissing games. I told her the mother was there the whole time, staying out of the way in the bedroom, of course, and she said, "That's exactly what I mean."

What kind of an answer is that? I don't get it. I don't get any of it. All I know is I can't eat what I want, wear what I want, keep my hair and my nails the way I want, keep my room the way I want or go where I want. So last night we really had it out.

"Listen!" I screamed at her. "You are not letting me have

any fun and I'm sick of it. You are always pushing me around and telling me what to do. How come nobody ever gets to tell *you* what to do, huh? Tell me that!"

She said, "Annabel, when you're grown-up, people don't tell you what to do; you have to tell yourself, which is sometimes much more difficult."

"Sounds like a picnic to me," I said bitterly. "You can tell yourself to go out to lunch with your friends, and watch television all day long, and eat marshmallows for breakfast and go to the movies at night . . . "

"And do the laundry and the shopping, and cook the food, and make things nice for Daddy and be responsible for Ben and you . . . "

"Why don't you just let me be responsible for myself?" I asked.

"You will be, soon enough," she said.

"Not soon enough to suit me," I snapped.

"Is that so!" she said. "Well, we'll just see about that!" and she marched out of the room.

* * * * * * * * * * * *

A. Talking about the story

1. Do you think Annabel is going to enjoy living her mother's life? Why or why not?

2. Three of the passages in this book so far, including this one, are written in the first person. Which passages are they?
   How does writing in the first person affect the way authors express themselves and the language they use?

B. Talking around the story

1. Annabel does not think she has enough freedom. Do you have the same complaints about the amount of freedom you are allowed at home?
   What sort of rules and regulations at home do you dislike most?
   Why do you think these rules exist?

2. Annabel has to eat school dinners, which she hates.
   What sort of lunches can you have at your school?
   Do you find the system satisfactory?
   If not, what would you prefer?

3. If you could swap lives with any other person in the world, who would you choose?
   Why would you choose that person?

C. Activity: interviewing

In earlier books in this series, you have interviewed people from your own class and younger children. You are now going to interview an adult.

This interview will have to be carried out for homework, but you can compose and organise your questions now.

Work in pairs. You will each need a pencil and paper.

You will be interviewing an adult you know well on the subject of "My Schooldays".
You should try to find out ways in which their life at school was different from yours.
With your partner, think up as many questions as you can. Try to encourage the adult to give full and interesting answers. Avoid questions which will get the simple answer of "yes" or "no". When you have decided on the questions, work out the best order to ask them in.

If you have a tape recorder at home, you could make a recording of the interview. In this case, do not forget to give a brief introduction of the person you are interviewing before you begin. If you do not have a tape recorder, you can make notes of the answers.

From the information you have collected, perhaps you could make a news-sheet called "Schooldays of the Past". If this could be duplicated, you could give a copy to each adult who has been interviewed.

Other Good Reads

For people who enjoy stories set in historical times, there are many fine historical novels written for your age group. As well as Geoffrey Trease, look out for Rosemary Sutcliffe. Her books are quite difficult to read but well worth the effort. *Eagle of the Ninth**** (Puffin), for instance, is an adventure set in Roman Britain where the Ninth Legion of the army has mysteriously disappeared in the northern marshes. Marcus, a young Roman centurion, sets off to search for traces of the Legion, particularly its standard, the Eagle.

In the opposite direction, there are many good stories of the future — science fiction. *Islands In the Sky*** by Arthur C. Clark (Puffin) is about Roy Malcolm who wins a trip to a space station. The station is described in fascinating detail, as are Roy's adventures aboard it.

Another good story of the future is Nicholas Fisk's *Time Trap*** (Puffin) in which the hero (a boy called Dano from AD 2079) finds a way of travelling in time. He comes back into the past, but also goes forward, and finds a terrifying future waiting for him.

A thoroughly contemporary novel, aimed at girls, is Judy Blume's *Blubber** (Piccolo). Blubber is the nickname given to a girl in Jill Brenner's class, whom everyone picks on and bullies. Judy Blume really seems to get inside the girls' minds — it's very realistic, and quite horrifying how nasty people can be to each other!

Also nasty is the theme of *How to Eat Fried Worms** by Thomas Rockwell (Piccolo). Billy is bet by his friend that he can't eat fifteen worms! If he can, he wins fifty dollars to buy a bike; if he can't, he loses face. A funny story.

Playing It Right** by Tony Drake (Puffin) is a book for cricket fans. The boys of Jubilee Street School begin a cricket team, and with some talented players they look set for success. But tensions develop between the boys, which might threaten the spin-bowler, Nirmal Singh. And then Colin and Trinton, the star players, are banned from the team on suspicion of burglary.

There is tension too in *A Cat Called Amnesia** by Nicholas Hildick (Knight), when the Bleeker family find a stray cat wandering near their holiday home. Mr Bleeker declares that it will have to be destroyed unless the owner can be found, so the four Bleeker children mount a complex detective operation to save the cat.

The animal hero of *Hound in the Highlands*** by Brenda Sives (Beaver) needs no human assistance. He is Sherlock Hound, and accompanied by Dr Winston (a shaggy sheepdog) he sets off to solve the mystery of the Phantom Piper at a remote and ancient castle in Scotland. If you enjoy this book look out for the follow up, *Hound and the Witching Affair.*

For good readers *Bridge to Terabithia**** by Katherine Paterson (Puffin) is a book with enormous impact. It begins as a slow-moving peaceful tale about an American country boy, his new friend Leslie, and the imaginary land they create. But the climax of the story comes suddenly like a punch in the face, and from then on it's a book you will never forget.

8 Terry on the Fence
by Bernard Ashley

Bernard Ashley is a headmaster of a junior school in South London. He wrote his first novel because "I needed something to do that would stop me worrying and being unhappy," and he found it worked. Since then he has written many successful books for young people. The idea for *Terry on the Fence* came from an experience in his own childhood, when some older boys ambushed him as he was walking home. Bernard Ashley loves football, and has written about football at school in his book, *All My Men*.

* * * * * * * * * * * *

Terry Harmer has just had a terrible row with his mother and sister, and has stomped out of the house in a rage. He runs away to the Common, intending to camp out for the night, to worry his parents. Then a thunderstorm breaks out, and Terry has to decide whether to go home and face a row, or to find somewhere to shelter, like the old bandstand on the Common . . .

He decided on the bandstand. He hadn't run off for nothing. There was a second's hesitation while he wondered whether or not it was safe from the lightning under there, but he guessed it had to be: they wouldn't be allowed to put them up without lightning conductors, or in a summer storm you'd see the bandsmen diving off in all directions to get away from their metal instruments.

With a sudden flash of lightning acting as a starting pistol he put his head down and began to run, spurred on by the following clap of thunder which echoed around the sky in a series of rippling cracks. He ran swiftly over the slippery grass towards his objective – the bare frame of ornate green ironwork which stood lifeless in the rain, waiting, like some huge shrub, to flower with colourful uniforms in the summer. He only just made it. The next flash, brighter than before, took the colour from the grass before him, and the deep boom that went with it with the awful finality of a hydrogen bomb, spurred him to leap up over the last metre of grass and land sprawling on the screeded floor of the bandstand. Panting, he scrambled to the centre of the concrete circle and crouched down beneath the tall and elegant metal canopy. He was soaking wet. His shirt clung coldly to the front of his body like a creased black skin, and his jeans clutched round his legs like wet hands. Another electric-white flash lit up the common and an instantaneous crash shook the earth. Terry screwed his eyes shut tight, terrified, as the elements demonstrated their huge power over the civilisation of south London, and the urgent hissing of the downpour sounded like silence in his ears when the thunder stopped.

Terry opened his eyes in time for the next bright flash, a jagged arrow which left a purple image on his retina. And then he saw them. Five faces, staring, smiling at him from the filled-in section of the bandstand, squirting derisive laughter at him in the huge wave of thundering sound.

His first reaction was to shut his eyes again, to tell himself that they weren't there. Surely he'd been alone on the common. But a second, deeper, instinct told him to get away, quickly. You didn't stop to argue with a gang of hostile

kids down here. In a fraction of a second he was on his feet
and running towards the bandstand steps – but swift as he
was, he hadn't the advantage of anticipation, and the others
had. One of them was blocking the only way off before he'd
gone two metres.

"Where you off to, Pig-face?" The voice was croaky, just
broken, but with a cat-and-mouse lilt to it.

"Duff him, Les!"

"Put yer boot in!"

"Gob on 'im!"

The chorus was giggled, but sinister.

"Shut yer mouths!" High, drawn out, and firm, the leader's
voice halted the suggestions.

Terry stared up into the strange and frightening face before him. Two slitted blue eyes held him there, a pair of flaking raised eyebrows and an open "what're-you-going-to-do-about-it" mouth, chin up in a mocking query, dared him to move. That close, and afraid to step back into the others behind him, Terry registered two other features in his frightened mind. The older boy's skin was paper-thin, drawn across his forehead like a very old man's, and the only hair he seemed to have grew in a thin dead lock high up on his head.

"Si' down. All of yer."

* * * * * * * * * * * *

A. Talking about the story

1. What do you think will happen to Terry now?

2. Before Terry meets the gang, there is a vivid description of his run through the storm into the "safety" of the bandstand. The author often achieves his effects by the use of comparisons. He says, for instance, that Terry's rain-soaked jeans "clutched round his legs like wet hands".
   Is "like wet hands" a good description? Why do you think it is or isn't?
   Find three more comparisons in the passage, and discuss how effective they are.

B. Talking around the story

1. Les and his gang have now got Terry in their power. They ask him all about his school, and decide to break into it and steal the valuables. They try to make Terry help them in this plan, saying they will beat him up if he doesn't.

If you were in Terry's situation, what would you do?
What problems would there be in the course of action you
have chosen?

2. Terry has run away from his problems at home. In *Underground to Canada* you read about slaves escaping. What is
   the difference between "running away" and "escaping"?

C. Activity: whodunnit?

This is a detective game.
The classroom is now a supermarket: tables are display cases
of food, bookcases are freezer cabinets, etc. Quickly label the
main areas of the supermarket, e.g. the check-out desk, the
meat counter, the dairy counter.

Six people are detectives. They must now go out of the room.
The rest of the class are shoppers in the supermarket, but one
is a murderer. Draw lots to choose who this will be. One slip
of paper should have an M on it. If you get this, you are the
murderer — *but do not let anyone guess it is you.*

Now everyone becomes a shopper in the supermarket, walking
around, choosing food, comparing prices, and so on.
The murderer should act as naturally as anyone else, until
there is a chance to murder someone. To do this, the murderer
catches the eye of the victim and secretly winks at him or her.
The victim must freeze like a statue immediately, and *close his
eyes.* The murderer will, of course, slip away as naturally as
possible.

The first person — and only the first! — to notice the body
(someone standing frozen with eyes shut) must scream. This
is the sign for the detectives to enter.

The detectives have eight minutes to find out who committed
the murder. To do this they must question all the people in
the supermarket.

Rules for questioning

1. Detectives may ask people where they were, what they noticed, etc., but they may not ask directly if a person knows who the murderer is.
2. No one may give any information unless they are asked for it.
3. Each detective must question as many people as possible — it does not matter that each person is questioned several times.
4. Everyone must tell the truth, except the murderer, who can lie as much as he or she likes.
5. At the end of the questioning, the detectives confer. They then have three guesses. If they guess correctly, the murderer must surrender. If not, the murderer has escaped.

When you have played the game once, discuss with your teacher how best to organise it in your classroom. Then try it again. You may have time to try it a few times.

9 The Ghost of Thomas Kempe

by Penelope Lively

Penelope Lively was born in Egypt and, "trapped by the war", lived there with her family until 1945 when they returned to England. She was twelve and had never been to school. Education material sent out from Britain often ended up sunk at the bottom of the Mediterranean. So she used to read a huge amount — a perfect background for a writer. She is fascinated by the idea of time, but dislikes stories where people go back into the past. In *The Ghost of Thomas Kempe* she explores how a seventeenth-century character reacts to the twentieth century.

* * * * * * * * * * * *

James Harrison, his parents and his bossy sister, Helen, have just moved into a creaky old cottage on the outskirts of Ledsham. James is very happy there, playing with his dog Tim and digging holes in the back garden to see what he can find, until strange things start happening around the cottage. Weird messages in old-fashioned writing begin appearing in unlikely places, and things start to bump about and go missing. James always gets the blame, especially when the chemist won't accept a prescription for some medicine for Helen because the phantom scribbler has been at it.

Later that evening, James tries desperately to stop Helen finding out that he didn't get her cough mixture. . . .

Television has many virtues, not the least of them being, James thought, that it provides a continuous noise to paper over a potentially unreliable situation. The Harrisons settled down for the evening: once, Helen said, "Where's my new cough mixture?" but her mother's reply was drowned in a burst of gunfire from the Mexican border.

"Ssh," said James. "This is good."

He and Helen lay on their stomachs, side by side, with Tim between them. Tim sat with his head between his paws, facing the television set, eyes half-closed, occasionally twitching. He clearly thought the television screen to be a window beyond which there was a real and thrilling world from which he was excluded, peopled with fleeing horses, other dogs, and a host of wild animals. Occasionally, when things got too much for him, he would hurl himself against the glass in an abortive attempt to chase these elusive creatures. He was believed by James and Mr Harrison to appreciate a good Western.

"Bed," said Mrs Harrison, at last.

"In a minute," said James and Helen in unison.

"As soon as the news is over, then."

The news ended. The weather forecast began. "Tomorrow will be cloudy and dull in most parts, with light to moderate winds. Temperatures will be around . . . "

There was a loud crash from the sideboard. Everybody looked round. The blue vase was lying on the floor in pieces.

"I didn't touch it," James said quickly. "I was over here."

"Nor me," said Helen. Both children looked at their mother with expressions of deep virtue.

"How very peculiar," said Mrs Harrison, picking up the pieces. "Luckily it's one I've never cared for. A wedding present."

"How on earth did it fall off by itself?" said Helen.

"Small local earthquake," said their father with a yawn. "Very frequent in this part of Oxfordshire. Up, both of you." He picked up the newspaper.

James and Helen climbed the stairs slowly, pausing on every step to argue about who was to use the bathroom first. At the top, Helen gave in unexpectedly.

"You have it. Anyway, you need it most," she added as an afterthought. Then, "I say, it was funny about that vase, wasn't it?"

"Mmm," said James, abstractedly.

"Didn't you honestly do it? Not with a string or something?"

"I jolly well did not."

"All right, all right. I just wondered."

James, feeling in his pocket for the various objects he had brought in from his hole, felt the rustle of a piece of paper and remembered. For a moment there flitted around in his head the notion of telling Helen about it, even showing her, telling her about the prescription ... There were times when she could be almost human, and he needed help. Then commonsense prevailed: this wasn't the kind of thing you let a mere girl in on, least of all Helen. He creaked up the stairs to his room.

He was a long time getting to bed. First of all he had to clear a shelf for his new treasures: the spectacle frame, the best of the clay pipes (one, indeed, intact except for an inch or so of stem), the pottery sequence, and various buttons and pieces of bone. He was planning a small exhibition, to be called "Three Hundred Years of Domestic Life in an Oxfordshire Cottage". Then, when he'd done that, there was the notebook to be filled in (under "Future Plans" he wrote in block capitals FIND OUT WHO IS PLAYING TRICKS ON ME AND JOLLY WELL SORT HIM OUT), and then at last he was able to get into bed.

He was lying there, telling himself a long and elaborate story about a shipwreck in which he was all the characters by turn, when it suddenly appeared to him that all was not right with the mirror above the table. There was writing on it. He shot out of bed and bounced across the room. Oh *no* . . .

There was a further message, scrawled greasily on the mirror in (oh, horror!) his mother's lipstick. James read it with a mixture of indignation and mounting amazement.

> We must take paines to informe thy neighboures that I doe once more practise my arte and cunninge in this howse. There is much businesse for us in the towne: I fancie manie doe practise witcherie. Tell thy familie they shall knowe what the weather will be from me & not from that eville machine or I will breake more pots. I perceive thou hast dygged up my spectacles & my pipe. It was my first apprentice loste them in the yarde: he was a scoundrell & a lazie fellow & I had often cause to beate him. Take care that thou serve me better.

A. Talking about the story

1. It seems that the ghost of Thomas Kempe was responsible for breaking the vase in the living room. Why did he do it?

2. (a) Why is Thomas Kempe's message in such strange language?
   (b) Apart from the peculiar spelling, what else is odd about what the ghost writes?

3. How well do you think James and his sister, Helen, get on? What part of the passage tells you this?

B. Talking around the story

1. Brothers and sisters often argue about little things.
   If you have a brother or sister, what do you argue about?
   Is there anything you like about your brother or sister?
   Is there anything you hate?
   If you don't have a brother or sister, would you like one?
   Why do you give this answer?

2. Although no one would believe James, the ghost in this book is real.
   Do you believe in ghosts? Why, or why not?
   Are there any ghost stories connected with your area? Tell the class about them.
   What sort of places might you expect to be haunted? Why?

C. Activity: any questions?

"Any Questions?" is a radio programme in which a panel of well-known people are asked questions by the audience. They are expected to give their opinions on anything the audience asks them. These questions are usually serious, but there is an occasional funny one.

You need a panel of four people and a chairman. The chairman's job is to decide who should ask the next question, and make sure that each member of the panel gets a chance to answer.

Each member of the audience should have a question ready. Here are some sample questions:

Do you think people spend too much time watching television?

Do you think it is better to live in the country or the town?

Do you think Enid Blyton is a good writer?

When a member of the audience has a question, he should put up his hand and wait for the chairman to invite him to speak. He should then stand up, state his name, and put his question clearly. Each member of the panel should give his opinions as clearly as he can.

When one panel has answered two or three questions, four other people can take over.

10 Ash Road
by Ivan Southall

Ivan Southall lives in New South
Wales, Australia. He started work
on a newspaper as an apprentice
engraver, but during the Second
World War became a pilot in the
Royal Australian Air Force. After
this he started writing novels for
young people. Some of his books
have been criticised by adults
because they are thought to be
too frightening for children. The
idea for *Ash Road* grew out of a
bush fire near his house which
destroyed many people and their
land, but which the Southalls
survived.

* * * * * * * * * * * * *

This story is set in Australia, in an area which, each
summer, is hot and dry and dusty. Great bush fires can
occur in this landscape, so strong and fast-moving that
they wipe out forests, farmland, townships, and people.

Wallace, Graham and Harry are on holiday for the first
time without their parents, camping in the bush. Although they've been warned of the danger of starting a
fire, they have bought a small heater, run on methylated
spirits, so that they can cook sausages at their camp.
When darkness falls they settle down to sleep . . .

Wallace was half-awake, half-asleep. He had been asleep for a while, but had become partly aware of his surroundings again, of the wind and the heat. He was wet with perspiration. Graham had been right about sleeping-bags and ovens. Wallace felt that he was being cooked, and his right hip was bruised and sore. He had dug a little hole for his hip, but he must have turned away from it. The trouble was, he couldn't completely wake up. He was in a sort of limbo of acute discomfort but was too hazy in the head to do anything about it.

When at last he managed to open his eyes he became aware of a faint glow. He thought he could smell methylated spirits. He even thought he could see Graham.

"Is that you?" he said.

"Yes," said Graham.

"What are you doin'?"

"Making coffee."

Wallace sat up, panting. He felt giddy. "What are you makin' coffee for?"

"I'm thirsty. Do you want a cup?"

"What's the time?"

"Twenty past one."

"Yeh. I'll have a cup."

Wallace peeled his sleeping-bag down to the waist, and felt better. "Twenty past one!"

"About that."

"Harry's sleepin' all right."

"Trust Harry," said Graham. "He could sleep anywhere."

Wallace thought he had heard something like that before, but couldn't remember when. "Funny in the bush at night, isn't it? Awful dark."

"Noisy, too. I heard a tree fall down. Not far away either. Woke me up."

"It's the wind."

"Guess so."

"Stinkin' hot, isn't it?"

"You can say that again. But this water's awful slow coming to the boil."

"The wind, I suppose."

"It's taken two lots of metho already," said Graham.

"Have you got the lid on?"

"Can't see when it boils if you've got the lid on."

"Put the lid on, I reckon, or it'll never boil."

"Don't know where the lid is, do you?"

"*Feel* for it. It's there somewhere. Use your torch."

"The battery's flat. Blooming thing. Must have been a crook battery. Hardly used it at all. *Now* look what I've done! There's the metho bottle knocked for six."

"You dope," cried Wallace. "Pick it up quick. Or we'll lose it all."

"The cork's in it." Graham groped for it, feeling a bit of a fool, and said, "Crumbs."

"Now what?"

"The cork's *not* in it, that's what. It must have come out."

"How could it come out? Honest to goodness – "

"It's *burning*," howled Graham.

A blue flame snaked from the little heater up through the rocks towards the bottle in the boy's hand; or at least that was how it seemed to happen. It happened so swiftly it may have deceived the eye. Instinctively, to protect himself, Graham threw the bottle away. There was a shower of fire from its neck, as from the nozzle of a hose.

"Oh my gosh," yelled Wallace and tore off his sleeping-bag. "Harry!" he screamed. "Wake up, Harry!"

They tried to stamp on the fire, but their feet were bare and they couldn't find their shoes. They tried to smother it with their sleeping-bags, but it seemed to be everywhere. Harry couldn't even escape from his bag; he couldn't find the zip fastener, and for a few awful moments in his confusion between sleep and wakefulness he thought he was in his bed at home and the house had burst into flames around him. He couldn't come to grips with the situation; he knew only dismay and the wildest kind of alarm. Graham and Wallace, panicking, were throwing themselves from place to place, almost sobbing, beating futilely at a widening arc of fire. Every desperate blow they made seemed to fan the fire, to scatter it farther, to feed it.

"Put it out," shouted Graham. "Put it out."

It wasn't dark any longer. It was a flickering world of tree trunks and twisted boughs, of scrub and saplings and stones, of shouts and wind and smoke and frantic fear. It was so quick. It was terrible.

"Put it out," cried Graham, and Harry fought out of his sleeping-bag, knowing somehow that they'd never get it out by beating at it, that they'd have to get water up from the creek. But all they had was a four-pint billy can.

The fire was getting away from them in all directions, crackling through the scrub down-wind, burning fiercely back into the wind. Even the ground was burning; grass, roots, and fallen leaves were burning, humus was burning. There were flames on the trees, bark was burning, foliage was flaring, flaring like a whip-crack; and the heat was savage and searing and awful to breathe.

"We can't, we can't," cried Wallace. "What are we going to do?"

They beat at it and beat at it and beat at it.

"Oh gee," sobbed Graham. He was crying, and he hadn't cried since he was twelve years old. "What have I done? *We've got to get it out!*"

Harry was scrambling around wildly, bundling all their things together. It was not that he was more level-headed than the others; it was just that he could see the end more clearly, the hopelessness of it, the absolute certainty of it, the imminent danger of encirclement, the possibility that they might be burnt alive. He could see all this because he hadn't been in it at the start. He wasn't responsible; he hadn't done it; and now that he was wide awake he could see it more clearly. He screamed at them: "Grab your stuff and run for it." But they didn't hear him or didn't want to hear him. They were blackened, their feet were cut, even their hair was singed. They beat and beat, and fire was leaping into the tree-tops, and there were no black shadows left, only bright light, red light, yellow light, light that was hard and cruel and terrifying, and there was a rushing sound, a roaring sound, explosions, and smoke, smoke like a hot red fog.

"No," cried Graham. "No, no, no." His arms dropped to his sides and he shook with sobs and Wallace dragged him away. "Oh, Wally," he sobbed. "What have I done?"

"We've got to get out of here," shouted Harry. "Grab the things and run."

"Our shoes?" cried Wallace. "Where are they?"

"I don't know. I don't know."

"We've got to find our shoes."

"They'll kill us," sobbed Graham. "They'll kill us. It's a terrible thing, an awful thing to have done."

"Where'd we put our shoes?" Wallace was running around in circles, blindly. He didn't really know what he was doing. Everything had happened so quickly, so suddenly.

"For Pete's sake run!" shouted Harry.

* * * * * * * * * * *

A. Talking about the story

1. (a) How exactly did the fire start?
   (b) Why did it spread so quickly?

2. The three boys differ in their reactions to the fire, once it
   has got out of control. How does Graham react? How does
   Wallace? What about Harry? Think of reasons why each
   boy reacts in that particular way.

B. Talking around the story

1. The boys have started a bush fire which sweeps through
   the countryside, and is responsible for the deaths of several
   people.
   Whose fault would you say it was?
   Could you blame it on any one person?
   If you decide anyone is responsible for the fire, would you
   say he was equally responsible for the deaths?

2. Because Australia is so hot and dry in the summer, there is
   always a danger of fire. This can lead to disaster. The
   climate and natural forces in other parts of the world can
   cause other types of disasters. Think of examples of these.
   Why do they happen?
   Are there any ways these disasters can be avoided?

C. Activity: a debate

A debate is a formal way of arguing a point.
The topic under discussion is called "the motion".
You are going to hold a debate on the motion that "Fireworks
are dangerous, and should not be sold to any member of the
public."

The teacher will choose two people to speak about the motion, one to speak in favour of it, and one to speak against. She will also choose a chairman, to be in control of the debate.

Everyone in the class will have a chance to speak on the subject eventually, so you should now all note down your ideas on it. You may find it helpful to work with a partner.

The speakers must quickly compile short speeches to put across the main points of their arguments. The teacher can help them.

When the speakers are ready, they should sit on either side of the chairman, in front of the rest of the class.
The audience in a debate is known as "the floor".

The chairman calls for order. He then introduces the speaker for the motion and invites him to speak. Any speaker in a debate must open his speech with the words "Mr Chairman (or Madam Chairman if it is a girl), ladies and gentlemen . . . "
The chairman then introduces the speaker against the motion and invites him to speak.

When the speakers have finished, the chairman opens the debate to the floor. The audience may now put their own points on the topic, or ask questions of the speakers. They must wait, however, to be invited to speak by the chairman, and they must remember to begin their speeches in the correct way.

At the end of the debate the chairman should call for a vote on the motion. If most people are in favour of the motion he announces that "the motion is carried". If most people are against it, he announces that "the motion is defeated".

Other Good Reads

Another book set in Australia is *Walkabout**** by James Vance Marshall (Peacock), in which Mary and her young brother Peter, find themselves stranded in the outback, miles from civilisation, after a plane crash. They have to survive and somehow find their way to safety in this harsh and terrifying countryside.

The threat of natural forces is also the theme of *Avalanche**** by Rutgers Van der Loeff (Puffin), set in Switzerland. Everyone who lives in the mountains is aware of the danger of avalanches, but this particular year, the avalanches are totally destructive. One buries a village alive, and attempts at rescue are hampered by the constant threat of more avalanches to come. The survivors are evacuated, often against their will, and are forced to leave behind trapped friends and relatives, not knowing whether they are alive or dead.

Set firmly in Britain and modern times is *My Mate Shofiq*** by Jan Needle (Fontana Lions). This is a powerful story of a Pakistani boy, Shofiq, and the problems his family has living in a northern town. Bernard doesn't think he likes "them" to begin with, but then he watches Shofiq beat off some bullies and is thrown into friendship with him. Their adventures are exciting and often disturbing.

The Great Gilly Hopkins** by Katherine Paterson (Puffin) is about a very badly-behaved girl who spends her time making life miserable for her teachers, social workers and foster parents. It seems impossible that Gilly can ever develop any feelings of kindness and responsibility until she arrives at kind-hearted Mrs Trotter's to be fostered. But by that time, maybe it's too late. . . .

The *Pippi Longstocking* books* by Astrid Lindgren (Puffin) are also about a girl: a very odd girl who lives in a cottage by herself, with a horse and monkey for company, and does exactly what she likes, when she likes. Her neighbours, Tommy and Annika, find her fascinating and exhilarating to be with and, since she's the strongest girl in the world, she can easily sort out any problems which arise. The first book is *Pippi Longstocking* and two follow-ups are available: *Pippi Goes Abroad* and *Pippi in the South Seas.*

Another fantasy is *The Eggbox Brontosaurus** by Michael Denton (Dragon); which is a hilarious modern fairytale. The hero, Prince Rudolf, sets off on a quest for enough cardboard eggboxes to build a giant model of a brontosaurus! But he is trailed by two evil villains, Gurp and Gawk, sent by his wicked stepmother to see he meets a sticky end.

If you prefer a more realistic adventure, look out for *The Hill of the Red Fox**** by Allan Campbell McLean (Collins Lions). The hero, Alasdair, becomes involved in a complicated adventure while on his way to stay with an uncle on the Scottish island of Skye. In the train, a strange man presses a note into Alasdair's hand, and is later found murdered. Is the man on the side of good or evil? What does his cryptic message mean? And is Alasdair's sinister uncle, Murdo Beaton, involved in the mystery?

A strange but fascinating book is *Mrs Frisby and the Rats of NIMH**** by Robert C. O'Brien (Puffin). Mrs Frisby is a mouse, living a comfortable mousy existence with her family, until their home is threatened with destruction. The mice have to seek help from a race of super-rats, who have escaped from a laboratory and are living in a super-den nearby. The adventures of the rats make gripping and exciting reading.

The last book we recommend is *Elidor**** by Alan Garner (Lions). Elidor is another world (mysteriously linked to Earth) where forces of evil have gained control. Four children slip, seemingly accidentally, into Elidor, and find themselves inextricably involved in its fate. The two worlds come closer, and the climax, as Elidorian evil lurches through the streets of Manchester, is a masterpiece of terror.